THOSE WHO HONOR ME

UNDERSTANDING THE WEIGHT OF HOLY THINGS

DR. DEBBIE RICH

debbie rich ministries

Those Who Honor Me: Understanding the Weight of Holy Things

ISBN 979-8-950602-00-9 (Paperback)

Invest in the Gospel

Invest in the Gospel: debbierichministries.org/give

CashApp: $DRMNATIONS

Venmo: @drmnations

PayPal: paypal.me/drmnations

Mail your gift to: Debbie Rich Ministries,
13194 US HWY 301 S. Suite #107 Riverview, FL 33578, USA.
Please make checks payable to Debbie Rich Ministries. *Thank you for your generosity!*

CONTENTS

INTRODUCTION

Honor is a subject of great importance to God. God will not bless a church, family, or individual who does not honor Him. Honor must be taught, because we need God to manifest Himself in a greater way, but there are principles we must understand to bring this about.

Recently, I celebrated 35 years of full-time ministry. I have observed those who honor God and those who do not. I have had meetings where people get a revelation of what it means to honor God, inviting His presence and yielding to it. Conversely, many have little understanding of what honor is, why we give it, or how we display it. When pastors and leaders lack understanding in this area, their congregants often have even less.

This book illustrates the contrast between honoring and treating sacred things lightly. Within these pages are biblical examples of both and their consequences. You will discover practical ways to demonstrate honor toward God and others. As a result, you will develop a clear understanding of honor and experience its rewarding results, recognizing that God honors you in proportion to your honor of Him.

I believe a new level of honor will flow forth from the Body of Christ, toward God and one another, which will invite an unprecedented manifestation of God's glory. May you be blessed as you read this book and apply its principles. Desire to be honored by Him and to learn all you can in this area, for God is pleased when you have a desire to honor Him. As you read, ask the Holy Spirit to illuminate your understanding and He will do so.

In Christ's Service,
DR. DEBBIE RICH

1

WHAT DOES THE BIBLE SAY ABOUT HONOR?

Honor seems to be an almost nonexistent virtue in the 21st century, particularly in Western society. Many have lost sight of its meaning. The anti-establishment rebellion of the 1960s dismissed traditional concepts of honor and rejected authority, rules, and morals. Flags and clothing were burned as people sought to dismantle hierarchies and establish a sense of equality, resembling a form of spiritual communism. However, the Bible reveals a clear distinction in position and rank, throughout society and within the Body of Christ. While we are equally loved, we have different callings and positions.

The Church of the Lord Jesus Christ should lead the way in restoring honor. It serves as an essential key to receiving from God and draws us closer to His heart, the source of all that is honorable. Honor helps us to become more like Him.

Honor can be defined as a good name or public esteem (reputation), a showing of respect or admiration, or adherence to what is right or a conventional standard of conduct. It represents high moral character, integrity, or a special distinction. The concept of honor can be applied in different situations, such as reverence, which implies profound respect mingled with love, devotion, or awe; or deference, which implies yielding or submitting to another's judgment or preference out of respect or reverence. Honor carries weight and depth; it is not a light or halfhearted thing.

God's glory and honor are interconnected, with some words in the Bible translated as "honor" and "glory" sharing similar meanings. Understanding honor provides insight into God, who is honorable in all things. The deeper your understanding of God's honor, the greater your comprehension of His glory.

Experiencing God's glory is, in essence, experiencing His honor. He honors us as we honor Him through spiritual hunger and yieldedness. His manifested presence is directly related to our honor toward Him. The ultimate expression of God's glory and honor is Jesus, the Word made flesh. Honor and glory were manifested in the flesh when Jesus came to the Earth, and He consistently conducted Himself with honor.

One honor principle is found in 1 Samuel 2:30:

> Wherefore the Lord God of Israel saith, I said indeed that thy house, and the house of thy father, should walk before me for ever: but now the Lord saith, Be it far from me; for them that honour me I will honour, and they that despise me shall be lightly esteemed.

The Hebrew word for *honor* here means, to be heavy, weighty, or to make honorable or glorious. This verse reflects two reciprocal actions: 1) honoring God and treating Him as weighty or precious brings divine honor, and 2) despising Him results in being lightly esteemed.

During Old Testament times, bartering served as the currency system. Transactions in the marketplace involved precious metals being used as a medium of exchange based on weight. When purchasing items, people would inquire about the cost in shekels, and the weight was balanced accordingly. For valuable items, merchants had to place a significant amount of gold or silver on the scale. They would retrieve a pouch of silver—often containing broken jewelry or silver rings—and weigh it on a two-pan balance scale until it matched the weight of the purchase. Heavier items were considered more valuable and thus commanded a higher price, while lighter items were considered inexpensive.

Biblically, the definition of honor is associated with the concept of weightiness. The Greek word for honor, *timē* (pronounced "tee-mee"), emphasizes valuing. It denotes something valuable, precious, and weighty, like gold. Other definitions of honor include appreciation, esteem, regard, and respect, mirroring biblical definitions of glory. To honor means, to value, to consider something precious, costly, or expensive, and to prize or revere it. When we treat God's things as precious, valuable, and important, He reciprocates by treating our things similarly.

The Hebrew word often translated as glory is *Kavod,* meaning weight or heaviness and signifying splendor, honor, or magnificence. It describes the majesty of God and the glory of Christ, reflecting God's infinite, intrinsic worth and His very substance. God's glory and His honor are closely related, as we only give to what we honor. When we esteem God's things as valuable, we are willing to pay any price to possess them in our lives.

In 1 Samuel 2:30, God promises to honor those who honor Him. We desire to be honored by God. Therefore, understanding what it means to honor Him is crucial.

The Bible likens the Kingdom of Heaven to a treasure, and also to the pearl of great price, as illustrated in Matthew 13:44–46:

> Again, the kingdom of heaven is like unto treasure hid in a field; the which when a man hath found, he hideth, and for joy thereof goeth and selleth all that he hath, and buyeth that field. Again, the kingdom of heaven is like unto a merchant man, seeking goodly pearls: who, when he had found one pearl of great price, went and sold all that he had, and bought it.

This passage speaks of a man who sacrificed everything for the pearl of great price—honoring, sacrificing, and procuring it. Likewise, God's Word should be this precious to us. Such value and appreciation cultivate faith, which is inseparable from honor. God seeks those who will esteem and honor His Word, even when delivered through human vessels. We should receive God's Word and acknowledge it as the life-changing truth it is.

Honor implies weightiness. We pay a high price for what we value and prize. God's value system differs greatly from the world's. His sense of honor is distinct, and we are to emulate Him.

> Luke 16:15b – But God knoweth your hearts: for that which is highly esteemed among men is abomination in the sight of God.

Honor is intrinsic to God, and understanding honor is crucial to understanding Him. We must pray for God to help us see things from His perspective. Our values and priorities must align with His. If God deems something valuable, we should too. However, if He considers something worthless, it should hold no value for us; we shouldn't even consider it.

> 1 Thessalonians 2:13 (NKJV) – For this reason we also thank God without ceasing, because when you received the word of God which you heard from us, you welcomed it not as the

> word of men, but as it is in truth, the word of God, which also effectively works in you who believe.

Paul thanks God because the church received the Word as God's own, not merely as the word of men. This is why it worked so powerfully in those who believed. We should honor God's Word enough to recognize it as God speaking. If the Lord Jesus stood before you and spoke, would you esteem His words any differently than if you heard them by the Spirit in church or read them in the Bible? We should not be distracted, restless, talkative, or texting during a service. If we make that adjustment, revelation will flow. It is remarkable how selectively some people listen, but we must remember it is the life-changing Word of God.

Everything God does should deeply resonate with us. Ignorance can prevent us from appreciating Him and His works. Therefore, we must grow in honoring God and recognize the importance of esteeming what belongs to Him.

NOTES

2
THE COST OF DESPISING HOLY THINGS

1 Samuel 2:30b – …and they that despise me shall be lightly esteemed.

In biblical times, the word "despise" didn't carry today's modern meaning. We often equate it with hating something and wanting nothing to do with it. However, in the Hebrew, it signifies to disesteem, hold in contempt, disdain, or treat as vile. Specifically, in this context, it refers to those who show contempt for God or treat Him with contemptuous neglect. The root word, *bazah,* describes a contemptuous attitude toward God's authority and honor. It describes a heart attitude or action that insults or undervalues God's holiness, authority, and honor. It is often contrasted with honoring Him.

Today, it could be likened to someone saying, "Whatever! It's just another church service. It's just an offering. It's just the Bible. It's just someone praying." Their attitude conveys it is no big deal to them.

We don't appreciate being dishonored, and God doesn't either. Sometimes, church attendees act as if the pastor should be grateful they even bothered to show up. They believe they need to be coddled and praised to ensure their return. However, God is not privileged to have us attend His house and worship Him. Instead, it's *our privilege* to come and worship God, hear His Word, and enjoy His presence. We owe God *everything* and must never take Him for granted.

The Lord doesn't want His holy things despised; it's a sin. His things and words are precious and should be treated accordingly. He said, "those who honor Me, I will honor, but those who don't, I will despise." Here, "despise" means to make light of, to disesteem, to regard as insignificant, to make nothing of something. The Bible uses it to describe a lack of appreciation or honor. We have several biblical examples of despising. Consider the story of Eli and his sons serving as priests.

> 1 Samuel 2:12–17 (NKJV) – Now the sons of Eli were corrupt; they did not know the Lord. And the priests' custom with the people was that when any man offered a sacrifice, the priest's servant would come with a three-pronged fleshhook in his hand while the meat was boiling. Then he would thrust it into the pan, or kettle, or caldron, or pot; and the priest would take for himself all that the fleshhook brought up. So they did in Shiloh to all the Israelites who came there. Also, before they burned the fat, the priest's servant would come and say to the man who sacrificed, "Give meat for roasting to the priest, for he will not take boiled meat from you, but raw." And if the man said to him, "They should really burn the fat first; then you may take as much as your heart desires," he would then answer him, "No, but you must give it now; and if not, I will take it by force." Therefore the sin of the young men was very great before the Lord, for men abhorred the offering of the Lord.

Eli had grown cold. Once upon a time he knew something about God, but his sons did not. They were the sons of Belial, another name for the devil. They stole the people's offerings and scorned the Lord's ordinances. Their actions caused the people to despise the Lord's offerings. It is important to view offerings correctly, as they are holy, and our honor of them greatly affects how we treat and present them. We do not demand, beg, or manipulate. We must treat the Lord's offerings with respect and honor. Despising the offering means having the attitude of, "What difference does it make if we give, or how much we give?" People act as if there is no God. If parents act like that, so will their children. As pastors treat these things, so will the church. The laity will reflect how their leadership honors God. We must live by example and teach people to treat the things of God with great respect and honor.

> 1 Samuel 2:22–30 (NKJV) – Now Eli was very old; and he heard everything his sons did to all Israel, and how they lay with the women who assembled at the door of the tabernacle of meeting. So he said to them, "Why do you do such things? For I hear of your evil dealings from all the people. No, my sons! For it is not a good report that I hear. You make the Lord's people transgress. If one man sins against another, God will judge him. But if a man sins against the Lord, who will intercede for him?" Nevertheless they did not heed the voice of

> their father, because the Lord desired to kill them. And the child Samuel grew in stature, and in favor both with the Lord and men. Then a man of God came to Eli and said to him, "Thus says the Lord: 'Did I not clearly reveal Myself to the house of your father when they were in Egypt in Pharaoh's house? Did I not choose him out of all the tribes of Israel to be My priest, to offer upon My altar, to burn incense, and to wear an ephod before Me? And did I not give to the house of your father all the offerings of the children of Israel made by fire? Why do you kick at My sacrifice and My offering which I have commanded in My dwelling place, and honor your sons more than Me, to make yourselves fat with the best of all the offerings of Israel My people?' Therefore the Lord God of Israel says: 'I said indeed that your house and the house of your father would walk before Me forever.' But now the Lord says: 'Far be it from Me; for those who honor Me I will honor, and those who despise Me shall be lightly esteemed.'"

This was all about honor. God told Eli he honored his sons above Him.

> 1 Samuel 2:31–36 (NKJV) – "'Behold, the days are coming that I will cut off your arm and the arm of your father's house, so that there will not be an old man in your house. And you will see an enemy in My dwelling place, despite all the good which God does for Israel. And there shall not be an old man in your house forever. But any of your men whom I do not cut off from My altar shall consume your eyes and grieve your heart. And all the descendants of your house shall die in the flower of their age. Now this shall be a sign to you that will come upon your two sons, on Hophni and Phinehas: in one day they shall die, both of them. Then I will raise up for Myself a faithful priest who shall do according to what is in My heart and in My mind. I will build him a sure house, and he shall walk before My anointed forever. And it shall come to pass that everyone who is left in your house will come and bow down to him for a piece of silver and a morsel of bread, and say, "Please, put me in one of the priestly positions, that I may eat a piece of bread." '"

People sometimes don't understand love. Divine love doesn't mean always giving in to people or doing everything they want. Love does what is *best* for you, even if you don't like it.

Eli should have been a stronger leader, especially considering his sons' fornication. He should have confronted them sternly: "I've heard disturbing rumors, and if they prove true, you will be removed from your priestly office. Confess and repent now, or I will remove you from the priesthood." They might have protested, worrying about their livelihood and reputation. However, these things *must* be addressed, even with family. Some might consider such action too harsh, but neglecting problems allows them to fester until divine judgment becomes inevitable. Eli's sons died on the same day, and Israel lost the ark of the covenant and the glory of God. That is true hardship.

Eli's weak leadership is a cautionary tale. Romans 11:22 tells us, "Behold therefore the goodness and severity of God." God is good, and He is also severe. People are not judged by God if they judge themselves in accordance with His Word. Love is central but sometimes love requires difficult decisions. Some may question the presence of love in such decisions but ought to instead question the presence of commitment.

Love compels us to act in someone's best interest, even if it leads to temporary unpopularity. We cannot allow people to do whatever they want. Sometimes, we must take necessary steps to save their ministries and, potentially, their lives. We must be strong enough to do right and speak truth, regardless of perception.

The opposite of honor is *despising*. Consider the contrasting responses of Jacob and Esau to God.

> Genesis 25:29–34 (NKJV) – Now Jacob cooked a stew; and Esau came in from the field, and he was weary. And Esau said to Jacob, "Please feed me with that same red stew, for I am weary." Therefore his name was called Edom. But Jacob said, "Sell me your birthright as of this day." And Esau said, "Look, I am about to die; so what is this birthright to me?" Then Jacob said, "Swear to me as of this day." So he swore to him, and sold his birthright to Jacob. And Jacob gave Esau bread and stew of lentils; then he ate and drank, arose, and went his way. Thus Esau despised his birthright.

Esau was a hunter, but he had evidently not been successful, and he was hungry. He saw his brother Jacob with a big pot of red soup that smelled and looked delicious. He said, "Feed me. I'm weak and about to fall over." Jacob, who was spiritually hungry for God and His promises, responded, "Sell me your birthright. This is going to cost you big-time, brother. I want your birthright. Then, you can have all the soup you want." Esau said, "Look, I am about to die, so what good is it to me?" He sold it to Jacob for some pottage and lentils, despising his birthright. He was despising something holy, for the Lord is the One who established the blessing.

> Hebrews 12:15–17 – Looking diligently lest any man fail of the grace of God; lest any root of bitterness springing up trouble you, and thereby many be defiled; lest there be any fornicator, or profane person, as Esau, who for one morsel of meat sold his birthright. For ye know how that afterward, when he would have inherited the blessing, he was rejected: for he found no place of repentance, though he sought it carefully with tears.

Verse 15 speaks of bitterness before it names Esau. We see from this passage that bitterness causes us to fall short of God's grace and then defiles us. Bitterness is the open door for spiritual defilement. Is there is *any* situation where it's all right to remain bitter? No, not one. Bitterness does not only defile the person who is bitter; it can be contagious, defiling people around them.

Esau probably allowed his foreign wives to bring in defiling attitudes and practices. The Hebrews were supposed to remain pure and only marry from within. Esau brought great grief to his parents by marrying foreign wives with false gods. As a result, there were probably many family arguments.

> Genesis 26:34–35 – And Esau was forty years old when he took to wife Judith the daughter of Beeri the Hittite, and Bashemath the daughter of Elon the Hittite: which were a grief of mind unto Isaac and to Rebekah.

Once bitterness opened the door, it caused Esau to commit more sin. Esau is described as a fornicator and profane person. Fornicators trade something pure for immediate but temporary fleshly fulfillment. They don't know the value of the body. These bodies are precious and valuable, not to be abused or given to just anyone. The body is to be reserved for the spouse. These things are *holy*. Esau traded God's blessing for a bowl of soup, not valuing that which was precious and holy.

When their father was close to death and

sought to bless Esau as the firstborn, Jacob tricked him again. Esau came into the tent crying. The Bible says he was rejected and found no place for repentance. When you disdain the things of God instead of honoring them, you risk losing them, and it may take a while to get back what you forfeited. You cannot take God, His anointing, or His call lightly. You mustn't take Him for granted, for it will cost you. Appreciate and esteem the things God has given you.

Jesus was not given the honor He deserved in His hometown. Look at Mark 6:4 (NKJV):

> But Jesus said to them, "A prophet is not without honor except in his own country, among his own relatives, and in his own house."

The key here is *honor,* and the lack thereof. They didn't honor Him. The Greek word is *atimos,* meaning, not showing respect or value, and treating as common or ordinary.

Jesus returned to Nazareth, the city where He grew up, and on the Sabbath, He joined God's people as they gathered. He stood up and read from the Book of Isaiah, as recorded in Luke 4:18–19:

> The Spirit of the Lord is upon me, because he hath anointed me to preach the gospel to the poor; he hath sent me to heal the brokenhearted, to preach deliverance to the captives, and recovering of sight to the blind, to set at liberty them that are bruised, to preach the acceptable year of the Lord.

The crowd had heard this passage numerous times, as it was one of the main prophetic texts speaking of the coming Messiah. They questioned why this untrained young local was reading the scripture rather than their seasoned rabbi. Then came the bombshell. As Jesus rolled up the scroll, He announced, as recorded in verse 21, "Today this Scripture is fulfilled in your hearing." He went on to tell of the great and mighty works wrought in other cities and closed with a strong prophetic message. They thought, *How preposterous!* They began to murmur among themselves, "This is Jesus! What is He saying? He played with my son and was in his Torah class. He worked with His father in the carpenter's shop and built the table we eat at every night. We watched Him sweat and have to take a nap when He was tired. Who does He think He is?"

They had formed a mental image of how

their Messiah would come, based on their understanding of Scripture. They awaited a great king, a powerful conqueror who would deliver them from Roman oppression and establish them as a nation. But when Jesus came as one of their own, raised in their schools and laughing in their streets, they couldn't grasp it. He was often surrounded by tax collectors and prostitutes. This was not the way they expected the Messiah to come.

Often, God will send you what you need in a package you don't want. You must see what He is doing with your *heart*, not your *head*. There must be a breath of the Spirit of God. So, when Jesus came on the scene as an untrained man from Galilee, they mocked Him.

Consider Simeon, who was also watching for the Messiah.

> Luke 2:25–32 (NKJV) – And behold, there was a man in Jerusalem whose name was Simeon, and this man was just and devout, waiting for the Consolation of Israel, and the Holy Spirit was upon him. And it had been revealed to him by the Holy Spirit that he would not see death before he had seen the Lord's Christ. So he came by the Spirit into the temple. And when the parents brought in the Child Jesus, to

> do for Him according to the custom of the law, he took Him up in his arms and blessed God and said: "Lord, now You are letting Your servant depart in peace, according to Your word; for my eyes have seen Your salvation which You have prepared before the face of all peoples, a light to bring revelation to the Gentiles, and the glory of Your people Israel."

Simeon recognized this one-month-old baby as the Messiah, yet the people of Nazareth refused to acknowledge Him. Even when He was thirty years old and performing signs and wonders, the Pharisees mocked Him. This is because God is *Spirit*, and those who seek to understand His ways must know Him through His Spirit, who reveals truth. Many do not receive from God because of this. You must perceive God's actions and recognize those He uses through the Spirit of God.

So, how do we honor God and His people? It begins with how you see, hear, and respond to things.

> Luke 8:18 (NKJV) – Therefore take heed how you hear. For whoever has, to him more will be given; and whoever does not have, even what he seems to have will be taken from him.

> Mark 4:24–25 (NKJV) – Then He said to them, "Take heed what you hear. With the same measure you use, it will be measured to you; and to you who hear, more will be given. For whoever has, to him more will be given; but whoever does not have, even what he has will be taken away from him."

The Bible repeatedly instructs us to pay attention to how and what we hear. Two people can attend the same service, yet one leaves feeling happy and blessed while the other is bored and receives nothing. The first person heard with respect and recognized God was speaking to him; he treated God's Word and the message as precious and valuable.

The honor of God is a significant theme in the Bible. You must recognize its importance to Him within the Word and not regard God's things or His people as common. Your interactions with people reflect your relationship with God. Some claim, "I don't have much respect or honor for people, but I do for God," but that is not how it works. If you say you love Him but not His people, the Bible calls you a liar. The same principle applies here: respect and honor for God are demonstrated through respect and honor for God's people.

Some are dismissive—"It's just another preacher giving another sermon!"—and fail to appreciate the word of life. Consequently, they lack the heart to understand and the faith to receive. Remember Jesus' words:

> Luke 8:18 – Take heed therefore how ye hear: for whosoever hath, to him shall be given; and whosoever hath not, from him shall be taken even that which he seemeth to have.

> Luke 6:38b – For with the same measure that ye mete withal it shall be measured to you again.

The degree of honor, faith, and respect you demonstrate directly influences the measure of blessing and revelation you receive.

NOTES

NOTES

3
WHAT HONOR LOOKS LIKE

One way to demonstrate honor is your willingness and availability for God to use you in any situation or place. This means being ready at any time to sing, preach, play an instrument, cast out devils, testify, witness, or fulfill any other task He calls you to. The Bible urges us to be ready in season and out. If preparation is needed, readiness is lacking. Recall the parable of the ten virgins from Matthew 25:1–13: five were wise and prepared, while five were foolish and unprepared. The Lord values readiness, and our part is simply to obey.

The parable of the talents in Matthew 25:14–30 further illustrates this point. The Lord expects us to honor what He has already entrusted to us;

otherwise, He will not grant us more. In fact, what we presently have will be taken away. Neglecting to honor and respect His gifts can result in their loss. We must appreciate, value, and utilize what He has given.

Those whom God uses in this hour are those who honor and treasure Him above all else. They value Him, His Word, and His Spirit. Do not compare yourself to others or dwell on what you lack. The Bible cautions us not to despise the day of small beginnings. Therefore, never operate in false humility by prefacing your words with phrases like, "I'm just going to try to share something; it probably won't change your life." Instead, declare with confidence, "What I have to give you will change your life because it is not the words of men but the Word of God."

Some of my greatest ministry advancements occurred because I was willing to be used even when I felt unprepared. I have been asked to preach with no advance notice, my heart pounding, and my mind filled with doubt. Yet, trusting that God saw potential where I saw inadequacy, I stepped into His anointing, and it yielded great results.

It is important to honor those in positions of authority, recognizing that God has placed them there. We should address those in the five-fold ministry according to the office God has called them to.

> Matthew 10:41 – He that receiveth a prophet in the name of a prophet shall receive a prophet's reward; and he that receiveth a righteous man in the name of a righteous man shall receive a righteous man's reward.

This principle extends to the other ministry offices as well. He who honors an apostle as an apostle will receive an apostle's reward, and he who honors a pastor as a pastor will receive a pastor's reward. The same holds true for evangelists and teachers.

Jesus made it clear that receiving His disciples was equivalent to receiving Him.

> Luke 13:35 – Behold, your house is left unto you desolate: and verily I say unto you, Ye shall not see me, until the time come when ye shall say, Blessed is he that cometh in the name of the Lord.

He implied that they would not perceive Him again until they honored those He sent in His Name, suggesting that He manifests Himself when we bless or honor those He sends.

> John 13:20 (NKJV) – Most assuredly, I say to you, he who receives whomever I send receives Me; and he who receives Me receives Him who sent Me.

> Matthew 10:40–42 (NKJV) – "He who receives you receives Me, and he who receives Me receives Him who sent Me. He who receives a prophet in the name of a prophet shall receive a prophet's reward. And he who receives a righteous man in the name of a righteous man shall receive a righteous man's reward. And whoever gives one of these little ones only a cup of cold water in the name of a disciple, assuredly, I say to you, he shall by no means lose his reward."

Consider replacing "receives" with "honor" in these verses: "He who honors you honors Me, and he who honors Me honors Him who sent Me. He who honors a prophet in the name of a prophet shall receive a prophet's reward. And he who honors a righteous man in the name of a righteous man shall receive a righteous man's reward. And whoever honors one of these little ones with only a cup of cold water in the name of a disciple, assuredly, I say to you, he shall by no means lose his reward."

You must recognize the inherent authority structure within the Kingdom of God. This structure begins with the Father and extends to Jesus, the One He sent and to whom He delegated all authority. The Lord values delegation and expects you to respect *those in positions of authority* as you would *Him*. Matthew 10:40 illustrates this: rejecting the Son equates to rejecting the Father, while accepting the Son opens the door to the Father. Therefore, how should you receive a guest minister sent by the Lord to the church? You should receive them as if you were receiving the Lord Himself; He takes it personally.

The story of the Shunammite woman in 2 Kings 4:8–17 demonstrates this. Verses 9 and 10 say she recognized Elijah was a holy man of God and desired his frequent visits. She honored and valued the anointing on his life, asking her husband to furnish a room for him to ensure his comfort. Her sole intention was to honor God by honoring Elijah. She sought nothing in return, yet God rewarded her faithfulness by granting her a son after years of barrenness. When you honor God, He honors you.

It matters how you treat prophets, righteous individuals, or even the seemingly insignificant. Kenneth Hagin, primarily a teacher, often ministered prophetically. Some congregations failed to recognize or receive his prophetic gifting, perceiving him only as a teacher. Therefore, they only benefited from his teaching ministry, missing the greater blessings God intended to bestow. Your receptiveness to a ministry gift or even a message determines what you gain from it. Too often, people approach church with the expectation of merely singing a few songs, listening to a sermon, and returning home. With such limited expectations, they limit what they receive. God has *more* in store for His people.

Another way we demonstrate honor is through our manner of address, offering dignity and respect. My late husband, a pastor who went to be with the Lord in 2020, often told his congregation, "If you address me simply as Bob, you will only receive the limited wisdom Bob possesses. However, if you call upon the office of pastor, you will receive what God imparts through that office." It is crucial to address men and women of God serving in their respective offices with the honor and respect their positions deserve.

Would you rather be addressed as "my good friend" or "that woman"? Some preachers even refer to the Bible as "that thing." You must be mindful of how you refer to things and people. I once heard a man say, "Well, I don't know what's in that thing there (referring to the Bible), I just know what I believe." People who make jokes about God's things and His people are bordering on blasphemy, and that is not okay! You shouldn't laugh at such jokes, lest you risk despising the holy things of God. Your honor for God is directly revealed in how you honor His people. You are to respect the position God has placed them in, or you disrespect the God who put them there.

If you honor something or someone, you refer to them with designations of honor. If you value your wife, you will not call her your "old lady." If you value your father, you will not call him your "old man." No child should call their mother by her first name. The Bible clearly states to honor your parents. You don't have to respect everything they say and do, but you must respect their position as your father and mother, or you dishonor God.

Children must be taught respect for their teachers, coaches, and all who are in authority. You should never call the police "pigs." The Bible calls people in civil positions of authority "ministers," and they should be shown due respect. We should say, "yes, sir" or "yes, officer." It is godly to refer to people with titles and say things like, "yes, ma'am," as it shows your respect for them. Some think using "Mr.," "Mrs.," or "Miss" is just a Southern custom. No, it's a biblical principle.

The Bible tells us to honor our elders, whether in age or position.

> 1 Timothy 5:1 – Rebuke not an elder, but intreat him as a father; and the younger men as brethren.

> Leviticus 19:32 – Thou shalt rise up before the hoary head, and honour the face of the old man, and fear thy God: I am the Lord.

Gray hair is sometimes described as a "crown of glory" gained through a righteous life. Some view the elderly as simply taking up space and believe they should get out of the way, forgetting that they too will be there someday. They disdain the wisdom, experience, and knowledge the elderly possess. Younger people ought to respect, honor, and glean from that knowledge. Learn to love listening to older people who have lived life and gained wisdom from it. Learn all you can from them.

Lester Sumrall understood this principle

well. As a young man in his early twenties, he sat at the feet of Smith Wigglesworth in England. While many other young ministers could have benefited from Wigglesworth's wealth of wisdom, most dismissed him as an old, gruff man. Wigglesworth told Sumrall he was his only visitor. Lester Sumrall recognized the significance of the man before him.

You must honor those who have served God and His people, laying down their lives for the Gospel. The Bible instructs to give honor to whom honor is due, but also to be no respecter of persons. How do you reconcile these two ideas? Does impartiality mean treating everyone identically? No. You mustn't treat people differently based on superficial factors like wealth or worldly success. However, you should show special honor and respect to those who have faithfully served God for decades, whose lives and commitment to ministry have impacted countless others. Providing them with special seating, for instance, so they don't have to stand in the rain, is an honorable gesture.

Furthermore, you should extend a special preference to every believer simply because they are a believer. You offer a cup of cold water not merely because someone is thirsty or has a need, but because they are a child of God.

> 1 Timothy 5:17–18 – Let the elders that rule well be counted worthy of double honour, especially they who labour in the word and doctrine. For the scripture saith, thou shalt not muzzle the ox that treadeth out the corn. And, The labourer is worthy of his reward.

This passage also refers to financial support. Some individuals and churches have honored older ministers by providing for their financial needs.

Submission to authority is another key aspect of true honor. If you claim to honor authority but refuse to submit to it, you deceive yourself. Show respect and honor to those whom God has placed over you, for in disrespecting them, you disrespect God. The centurion in Matthew 8 understood and exemplified this principle.

> Matthew 8:8–10 – The centurion answered and said, Lord, I am not worthy that thou shouldest come under my roof: but speak the word only, and my servant shall be healed. For I am a man under authority, having soldiers under me: and I say to this man, Go, and he goeth; and to another, Come, and he cometh; and to my servant, Do this, and he doeth it. When Jesus heard it, he marvelled, and said to

> them that followed, Verily I say unto you, I have not found so great faith, no, not in Israel.

He understood submission to Jesus' word because, as an officer in the Roman army, he had men both above and beneath him in rank. Because he was quick to honor Jesus and submit to His word, he received what he sought.

What about when leaders are acting unrighteously or in an ungodly manner? In Acts 23, Paul was taken into custody, and Ananias commanded that he be struck. After Paul was hit, he responded, "God will strike you." Understandably, Paul was angry, as anyone would be who had been unlawfully struck. He called Ananias a whitewashed wall, but when others told Paul that he shouldn't speak to the high priest in that way, Paul said he didn't recognize him as the high priest and apologized. This was a godly thing to do, considering that the priest was abusing his position and had treated Paul unjustly. Yet, Paul apologized for his disrespectful language.

The Bible says King Saul was tormented by an evil spirit and became full of hate, jealousy, and bitterness because of the anointing on David. Though David tried to calm him by playing music, Saul sought to kill him, even throwing a spear at him. David ran for his life, hid in caves, and was treated like a criminal. Despite having an opportunity to kill Saul, David refused, stating he would not harm God's anointed. Saul was a demon-possessed man full of hate and murderous intent, but David still called him God's anointed because Saul had been chosen and anointed by God. David honored Saul for *God's* sake, not Saul's.

When someone is behaving inappropriately or doing wrong, you must maintain respect for their position. We may not respect everything they do, but we respect that God allowed them to be placed in that position. Those elected to office, such as presidents and senators, should receive a certain amount of respect. However, when they make laws contrary to God's Word, you must draw a line and refuse to compromise. Daniel was ordered not to pray, but he opened his window, and all could hear him praying.

Another way to show honor is by preferring others over your own desires. This might mean giving someone the better seat or recognizing that their time is more valuable than your own. Defer to those with greater anointing, and the younger should defer to the older. Ask, "What would you like to do?" Your needs and wants can wait and take a back seat to the one you are honoring. When they are talking, you don't need to talk. Instead, choose to go where they want, eat what they enjoy, and do what they like to do. When I am with generals of the faith, I say very little at their table, preferring to learn from them, follow their lead, and discern when to speak and when to listen.

Preferring one another means recognizing their worth in the Kingdom of God and treating them as though they are more important than you are. They are *not* more important, but you choose to *treat* them that way. It also means treating God's things as special. I don't throw my Bible in a magazine rack; it is valuable, as are my notes. They represent a lifetime of study and deserve preferential treatment.

Whatever you do for God's people, He will take personally. Today's society is fast-paced and people no longer want to take time to help one another, but God is watching. I know of a godly young lady who had car trouble and couldn't find anyone at church to help her. It was late at night, and it was not safe to walk anywhere. Even the usher wouldn't help.

One of my Bible school teachers told a story about when his car broke down. He went to six different places, about a mile apart, and no one would help him until he came to one home. The homeowners were of a different denomination and skin color, but when they found out this couple in need were Christians, they were so hospitable, bringing them in and building a fire in their little mobile home. They didn't have a phone but drove them to one. When the thankful couple tried to pay them, they said, "No, we're Christians and you are Christians. If we can't help each other out, what is life all about?" Yes, we should give one another preferential treatment, loving each other to such a degree that others desire what we have simply because of our love and honor.

Dr. Sumrall, now in Heaven, once explained that his "Feed the Hungry" program intentionally focused on feeding Christians. While this decision was controversial, it was rooted in the biblical principle of prioritizing love within the Body of Christ. Dr. Sumrall aimed to illustrate that serving the wrong god yields the wrong results, emphasizing the importance of supporting our fellow believers first. While I fully support outreaches to reach the lost, some Christians treat unbelievers with more love and honor than they show their own brothers and sisters in faith. You must begin by showing honor within the Body of Christ.

This honor should extend to financial

blessings. One way to honor God is through your finances.

> Proverbs 3:9 – Honour the Lord with thy substance, and with the first fruits of all thine increase.

Your financial choices reveal your values. Some demonstrate that money holds more value to them than God. Seize every opportunity to honor God with offerings. Money represents your time, blood, sweat, and tears; therefore, how you use it reflects your heart and desire to honor God. Prioritize Him in your finances. You also honor God by giving to others. You mustn't offer God or people your leftovers. God may ask you to give your "Isaac," your most cherished possession, to someone. When you do, He will honor you and care for your finances. You only give to what you value and honor.

I will never forget an experience during a ministry trip to Ukraine in 1998. A poor woman approached me with a translator, carrying a single fork and a broken locket. With tears streaming down her face, she explained, "These are the two most precious things I own, and I want to give them to God and to you tonight." Though inexpensive and broken, the locket represented her best, and I was deeply moved, weeping alongside her. Upon my return the following year, I learned she was prospering, had started a business, and was healed of breast cancer the very night she honored God with her best.

Such sacrifice reminds me of the story of the breaking of the alabaster box in John 12:1–8.

> Then Jesus six days before the passover came to Bethany, where Lazarus was, which had been dead, whom he raised from the dead. There they made him a supper; and Martha served: but Lazarus was one of them that sat at the table with him. Then took Mary a pound of ointment of spikenard, very costly, and anointed the feet of Jesus, and wiped his feet with her hair: and the house was filled with the odour of the ointment. Then saith one of his disciples, Judas Iscariot, Simon's son, which should betray him, Why was not this ointment sold for three hundred pence, and given to the poor? This he said, not that he cared for the poor; but because he was a thief, and had the bag, and bare what was put therein. Then said Jesus, Let her alone: against the day of my burying hath she kept this. For

> the poor always ye have with you; but me ye have not always.

Mary wanted to honor the Lord by taking the most expensive thing she had—costly perfume worth a year's wages—and pouring it on Jesus. He couldn't wear it or eat it; He couldn't build a church with it or launch a crusade. Yet, it was Mary's worship. Judas, a thief, led the way in dishonoring and disdaining the Lord, calling it a waste. It's no wonder he and the other disciples couldn't stand firm days later when the Lord was crucified; they didn't value Him as they should.

Even today, there are people who dislike the idea of offerings or people being honored through them. They have the spirit of Judas. Desire to have the spirit of Mary, who was simply pouring her love and honor on the Master and anointing His body for burial. Jesus praised her and prophesied that her beautiful act of honor would be shared everywhere the Gospel is preached. We still honor her today by telling this story. Her desire was to honor the Master, but this outpouring of anointing positioned her to be honored by the Master. The honor principle will *always* apply. The giving of gifts and offerings shows honor and love.

Recall our foundation verse, 1 Samuel 2:30:

> Wherefore the Lord God of Israel saith, I said indeed that thy house, and the house of thy father, should walk before me for ever: but now the Lord saith, Be it far from me; for them that honour me I will honour, and they that despise me shall be lightly esteemed.

This verse tells us that when we honor God, He honors us. Similarly, John 12:26 says:

> If any man serve me, let him follow me; and where I am, there shall also my servant be: if any man serve me, him will my Father honour.

This is reminiscent of Elisha following Elijah, declaring, "Where you go, I will go." On the day Elijah was to be taken up, he told Elisha to stay behind, but Elisha refused. This illustrates the heart of someone fully committed and sold out. There will be times when those you serve under, such as your pastors, might say, "It's okay, you can quit and go home." However, a committed heart will respond, "No, not until it's done." This is *honor*. Jesus said wherever He goes, His servant will be. Honor is found in obedience—

fully following God and those He has placed over you as they follow Christ.

If you desire God's glory, you must also desire His honor, as they are inseparable. The universal law of sowing and reaping applies here: if you honor Him, He will honor you. You will know it! *Everything* will return to you. If you sow honor and respect, honor and respect will be given to you.

Some lament, "No one is nice to me. No one gives me honor. No one sows into me." Do they sow these things into others? Are they faithful, loyal, and a good friend? Knowing I need faithful partners in ministry, I have purposefully sown faithfully into others.

Another way to show respect for God is by focusing on His work and avoiding impatience. Spiritual development requires concentrated focus. I once heard a minister recount a time when he felt it was time to leave a service. He was at a prayer meeting that he felt was going on too long. The Lord asked him, "What are you in such a hurry to leave and go to? You want to run from prayer to the late news and a sandwich." While it's true that some preachers can prolong services unnecessarily, remain reverent and avoid leaving for something less important.

NOTES

4
THE HONOR DUE HIS TABLE

We are taught to honor the Lord's table and understand the significance of the elements. Nothing should be honored more than the blood and body of Christ.

> 1 Corinthians 11:20–34 – When ye come together therefore into one place, this is not to eat the Lord's supper. For in eating every one taketh before other his own supper: and one is hungry, and another is drunken. What? have ye not houses to eat and to drink in? or despise ye the church of God, and shame them that have not? what shall I say to you? shall I praise you in this? I praise you not. For I have received of the Lord that which also I delivered unto you, that the Lord Jesus the

same night in which he was betrayed took bread: and when he had given thanks, he brake it, and said, Take, eat: this is my body, which is broken for you: this do in remembrance of me. After the same manner also he took the cup, when he had supped, saying, this cup is the new testament in my blood: this do ye, as oft as ye drink it, in remembrance of me. For as often as ye eat this bread, and drink this cup, ye do shew the Lord's death till he come. Wherefore whosoever shall eat this bread, and drink this cup of the Lord, unworthily, shall be guilty of the body and blood of the Lord. But let a man examine himself, and so let him eat of that bread, and drink of that cup. For he that eateth and drinketh unworthily, eateth and drinketh damnation to himself, not discerning the Lord's body. For this cause many are weak and sickly among you, and many sleep. For if we would judge ourselves, we should not be judged. But when we are judged, we are chastened of the Lord, that we should not be condemned with the world. Wherefore, my brethren, when ye come together to eat, tarry one for another. And if any man hunger, let him eat at home; that ye come not together unto condemnation. And the rest will I set in order when I come.

The Corinthian church was not honoring the Lord when they received communion. They were partaking irreverently, getting drunk, and engaging in gluttony. They came to eat and party, oblivious to the needs of others around them. Paul stated they would be guilty of dishonoring the body and blood of the Lord. They were becoming sick and dying prematurely because of their failure to esteem and honor the elements of the Lord's Supper. It would have been better for them not to gather than be irreverent.

Verse 27 has been frequently misunderstood, with many focusing on the question, "Am I worthy?" However, the emphasis is not on individual worthiness, but on the way you partake. You are not to take communion in an unworthy manner; rather, partake worthily by ensuring your sin is under the blood, asking Jesus to forgive you, and understanding what is available to you through the broken body and blood of our Savior.

Continually remind yourself that His broken body has provided healing for you, and His blood will make you whole, clean, and righteous as though you had never sinned, regardless of your past. Everything you need has been bought and paid for with the blood of Jesus Christ, and you must honor and respect His blood. When you honor His broken body, you can be healed immediately. You honor Him by mixing faith with what He has done for you and receiving all He has purchased for you. This must never become old and routine to you.

NOTES

NOTES

5
HONORING AND REVERENCING GOD

One of the most poignant stories about honor is found in 2 Samuel 23:14–17:

> And David was then in an hold, and the garrison of the Philistines was then in Bethlehem. And David longed, and said, Oh that one would give me drink of the water of the well of Bethlehem, which is by the gate! And the three mighty men brake through the host of the Philistines, and drew water out of the well of Bethlehem, that was by the gate, and took it, and brought it to David: nevertheless he would not drink thereof, but poured it out unto the Lord. And he said, Be it far from me, O Lord, that I should do this: is not this the blood of the men that went in

> jeopardy of their lives? therefore he would not drink it. These things did these three mighty men.

While David was staying in a stronghold during a war with the Philistines, he expressed a longing for water from his hometown well in Bethlehem. He wasn't giving an order or even making a request; it was more like thinking aloud. Yet, three of his mighty warriors broke through enemy lines to retrieve it. Two fought while one drew the water, and then they fought their way back. These men of God wanted to honor their leader and their God. Some might call it foolish to risk one's life for a cup of water, but that reveals a lack of understanding of honor.

David meant so much to these men. He had taken them in when no one else wanted them. They were the rejects of society, burdened with debt. No one believed in them but David. He told them they were somebody and they were important to him and God. He trained them, believed in them, fought alongside them, and stood with them. They would do *anything* for him.

They broke through the enemy line and returned bloody, scraped, and sweating, bringing the king his desire. "King David," they said, "we heard you long for a drink from the well of Bethlehem, so we brought you some." What happened next is incomprehensible to someone who does not understand honor: David poured out the water to the Lord. He essentially said it represented the blood of the men who had risked their lives for him, and he refused to drink it. He poured out the water to honor his men's bravery and devotion, rather than simply consuming it for his own comfort.

Some might think it's terrible they risked their lives for something he would not drink. However, this act should deeply move you! David was saying the water was too precious and valuable to drink, and he offered it to the Lord. He lifted it up to the Lord as they bowed their heads and knees, saying, "Lord, I'm giving this to You." David transformed a personal desire into an act of worship to God, signifying that such loyalty belonged to the Lord. This act of honor and worship to God and toward one another should teach us many points about honor. Never forget those who helped you, taught you, saw potential in you, and loved you.

There is a great lack of loyalty and honor within the Body of Christ today. Many individuals are aided, platformed, and introduced to ministry by others but allow offense and pride to obscure the role those individuals played in their beginnings. They forget God used those people to bring them to where they are today. Always remember those who have encouraged you, taught you, and imparted the anointing that transformed your life. Everyone is human, and unintentional hurts are inevitable, but endeavor to overlook offenses and remain committed to the people and ministries that have changed your life. The only justifiable reason to sever ties is when someone abandons Christ or His Word.

Most importantly, honor the precious Holy Spirit. Always speak to Him and about Him with the utmost reverence and honor. Whenever His presence, His Word, or the blood of Jesus is mentioned, show respect.

As the Church grows in these areas, God will be more evident among His people. Your praise, worship, and giving should come from the depths of your heart, directed to the Lord. Desire the Holy Spirit's powerful presence; honor and respect Him. While humor and enjoyment are welcome, you mustn't mock anything within the Church or make light of sacred things.

Desire for God to feel comfortable manifesting Himself among us, and when He does, He will bless us abundantly. May He find our churches to be places where He can easily manifest Himself, because we reverence and respect Him.

Much of the honoring and preferring of one another has been lost in recent years. The Church often swings between extremes. Some treat leaders as gods, while some leaders demand reverence, acting as though you must seek their permission for every action. Many simply seek to impress others, desiring constant attention and borderline-worshipful admiration, which becomes idolatry within the Church. This extreme is as detrimental as showing no honor at all. It is not about pride or bowing down to a person, but rather, the biblical principle of honoring God and His people.

Honor is displayed through actions, words, and thoughts. True honor originates from the heart. This is why God says in Isaiah 29:13:

> Therefore the Lord said: "Inasmuch as these people draw near with their mouths and honor Me with their lips, but have removed their hearts far from Me, and their fear toward Me is taught by the commandment of men."

True honor flows from a heart that fears God.

These things are holy to the Lord, and honor is *essential* to receiving from Heaven. Those who honor God will be honored. All who honored Jesus received from God in proportion to the honor they gave.

As you grow in awareness of your daily interactions with God and His people and intentionally choose to show honor, you can be confident God will honor you more. Therefore, I encourage you from this day forward to honor God in how you refer to Him and His people. Honor His Word and His Spirit. Focus on His presence, give preference to elders and those in authority, and give financially to honor God and His people. Remember those who have helped you and show honor for God's table in communion. Above all, honor the Holy Spirit in everything. He will then honor you with His presence and glory.

NOTES

POSTSCRIPT

Thank you for reading. I pray these pages transform your life beyond what you could have asked, thought, or imagined, as you apply the teachings within.

We would love to hear from you. If you were challenged to change and allow God to do His work in you, we pray that God would use you in a special way to touch a lost and dying world.

Write to us:
Debbie Rich Ministries
13194 US HWY 301 S. Suite #107
Riverview, FL 33578, USA

Email us:
office@debbierichministries.org

If you desire to see others find this teaching, you can write a review on Amazon or Goodreads, send a copy of this book to someone, or share about your experience on social media. The fruit of such seeds will go to your account in eternity. Thank you, and God bless you!

ABOUT THE AUTHOR

Dr. Debbie Rich is a renowned international teacher, evangelist, and revivalist who has carried the fire of revival to 55 nations and counting. Known for her fiery preaching and the move of the Holy Spirit, Dr. Debbie ministers with passionate boldness, igniting hearts to pursue holiness and the supernatural reality of God's presence.

She began her journey as a young believer baptized in the Holy Spirit. She trained extensively, attending Open Bible College in Des Moines, Iowa, and graduating from Rhema Bible Training Center in Broken Arrow, Oklahoma. Dr. Debbie earned her Ph.D. in Theology from Life Christian University, equipping her for anointed teaching and leadership.

As a pioneer missionary, she boldly ventured into the remote and challenging regions of the Alaskan Bush, where she nurtured groundbreaking revival fires and led a successful prison ministry that transformed many lives. Her fearless commitment to God's call propelled her to plant FaithLife Church and establish Word & Spirit Institute Northwest in Washington State. She is a sought-after teacher in Bible schools worldwide.

Currently based at Revival Ministries International in Tampa, Florida, alongside Drs. Rodney and Adonica Howard-Browne, Dr. Debbie continues to stir the Church to a deeper hunger for revival, empowering believers to encounter the Holy Spirit and walk in the fullness of God's holiness.

For over 35 years of full-time ministry, Dr. Debbie has sought to revive and embolden the Church with powerful messages, such as: keys to breakthrough in giving, the precious power from the breaking of the alabaster box, true and fervent spiritual hunger, and revival as a way of life. These teachings have transformed lives and continually made room for the Spirit of God to touch, heal, and strengthen the Church.

Her heart beats for the nations, for a Holy Ghost fire to sweep across the Earth, and for the

Church to rise as vessels of honor, sanctified and prepared for every good work. Through her ministry, countless lives have been set free, healed, and transformed by the power and love of Jesus.

CONNECT

Please visit debbierichministries.org to see upcoming events and announcements. You can find information about Debbie Rich Ministries on our website if you would like to learn more. You can also find our services on our website, Facebook, and YouTube.

Instagram: @debbierichministries
Facebook: @DRMDebbieRichMinistries
YouTube: @DebbieRichMinistries

OTHER BOOKS BY DR. DEBBIE RICH

Resurrected: Overcoming Death, Destruction and Defeat
Giving: Your Key to Breakthrough
Desperate Hunger Gets God's Attention
Undefiled
What Is Your Spiritual DNA?

THE HARVEST OF SOULS

We are soul winners, carrying the boldness of the Holy Ghost and compassion for the lost. You are called and you are equipped. Will go you forth?

The Great Commission, "Go ye into all the world and preach the Gospel to every creature," is for every believer to take personally. Every believer is to be an announcer of the Good News Gospel. When the Gospel is preached, people have an encounter with Jesus. Jesus is the only One who can change the heart of a man, woman, child, and nation!

This has nothing to do with personality or how comfortable we feel witnessing. We are *all* to be soul winners and tell people this Good News Gospel. Politics, religion, and good deeds cannot change the hearts of people.

At the end of this book is a tool to assist you in sharing the Gospel with others: "The Gospel Soul-Winning Script." Please make copies of it, and read it to people. As you read it to others, you will see many come to Christ, because as stated in Romans 1:16, "For I am not ashamed of the gospel of Christ; for it is the power of God unto salvation to every one that believeth…"

Drs. Rodney and Adonica Howard-Browne of Revival Ministries International have graciously made this Gospel Soul-Winning Script and many other soul-winning resources freely available to the Body of Christ.

When you have a revelation of this mandate from Heaven, you will use *everything* at your disposal to win souls. Please visit revival.com, click on Soul-Winning Tools, and review the many tools and videos that are freely available to help you bring in the harvest of souls. It is harvest time!

JESUS SAVES • JESUS HEALS • JESUS DELIVERS

SOUL-WINNING —SCRIPT—

Has anyone ever told you that God loves you and that He has a wonderful plan for your life? I have a real quick, but important question to ask you. If you were to die this very second, do you know for sure, beyond a shadow of a doubt, that you would go to Heaven? [If "Yes"— Great, why would you say "Yes"? (If they respond with anything but "I have Jesus in my heart" or something similar to that, PROCEED WITH SCRIPT) or "No" or "I hope so" PROCEED WITH SCRIPT.]

Let me quickly share with you what the Holy Bible reads. It reads "for all have sinned and come short of the glory of God" and "for the wages of sin is death, but the gift of God is eternal life through Jesus Christ our Lord". The Bible also reads, "For whosoever shall call upon the name of the Lord shall be saved". And you're a "whosoever" right? Of course you are; all of us are.

continued on reverse side—

JESUS SAVES • JESUS HEALS • JESUS DELIVERS

JESUS SAVES • JESUS HEALS • JESUS DELIVERS

I'm going to say a quick prayer for you. Lord, bless (FILL IN NAME) and his/her family with long and healthy lives. Jesus, make Yourself real to him/her and do a quick work in his/her heart. If (FILL IN NAME) has not received Jesus Christ as his/her Lord and Savior, I pray he/she will do so now.

(FILL IN NAME), if you would like to receive the gift that God has for you today, say this after me with your heart and lips out loud. Dear Lord Jesus, come into my heart. Forgive me of my sin. Wash me and cleanse me. Set me free. Jesus, thank You that You died for me. I believe that You are risen from the dead and that You're coming back again for me. Fill me with the Holy Spirit. Give me a passion for the lost, a hunger for the things of God and a holy boldness to preach the gospel of Jesus Christ. I'm saved; I'm born again, I'm forgiven and I'm on my way to Heaven because I have Jesus in my heart.

As a minister of the gospel of Jesus Christ, I tell you today that all of your sins are forgiven. Always remember to run to God and not from God because He loves you and has a great plan for your life.

[Invite them to your church and get follow up info: name, address, & phone number.]

Revival Ministries International
Please, register as a Soul Saving Station at revival.com/JoinS3 and log your soul count regularly.

JESUS SAVES • JESUS HEALS • JESUS DELIVERS

Made in the USA
Coppell, TX
09 June 2026

78687946R00049